Jumpstart the Creativity in Your Writing:

Tools for Writers at All Stages

By Mary Beth Magee

Published by BOTR Press, LLC
Poplarville, MS

All rights reserved. No part of this book may be used or reproduced by any means, graphic, electronic or mechanical, including photocopying, recording, taping or by any information storage electrical system without the written permission of the author except in the case of brief quotations embodied in critical articles and reviews.

ISBN: 978-1-7347101-8-2

Copyright 2021   Mary Beth Magee
Published by BOTR Press, LLC
www.BOTRPress.com

Cover photograph by Daniel@bestjumpstartreview
on unsplash.com
Graphics by Mary Beth Magee

This is an original work based on the author's research and personal experience.

Jumpstart the Creativity in Your Writing:

Tools for Writers at All Stages

By Mary Beth Magee

Dedicated to the many writers in all genres I have come to know and love. You have brought me a lifetime of delight – keep up the good work!

Contents

Forward	1
Introduction	3
What is Creativity?	5
A Formula for Creativity	9
On Inspiration	11
Inspiration	13
Sources of Inspiration	15
Collect things	15
Photograph places, people and things.	20
Copy things	24
Study things	28
Listen to inspiring music	31
On Imagination	33
Imagination	35
Read	38
Visit	41
Attend	44
Borrow Ideas from the Arts	47
Observe	51
Play	55
"What If?" the Situation	59

- Beyond "What If?" 64
  - Laugh often 67
- **On Information** 71
- **Information** 72
  - Reading 72
  - Experience your world 75
  - Write it down 78
  - Record your idea fragments 80
- **Start Creating** 82
- **Appendix** 84
  - *The Creativity Bill of Rights* 85
  - A Few Suggested Games 87
  - Creativity Exercises 88
  - Some Suggested Reading 90
  - To Hercules 92
  - Photo Credits 93
  - Books by Mary Beth Magee 94
  - Connect with Mary Beth Magee 97
  - Where to Find Books by Mary Beth Magee 98
  - End Notes 99

Forward

One of the most frequent questions I get as a writer is "Where do you get your ideas?"

The simplest, most truthful answer would be "Where don't I get them?"

Creativity comes from many places, many sources. As writers, we should keep an eye out for sparks of creativity everywhere we go. Those sparks will charge our creative batteries and help us write the next line, the next chapter, the next article, the next book.

This book is a writer-specific expansion of *Creativity: An Essential Tool for the Real World*, a general audience book I wrote to accompany the business workshops I lead. I hope you will find the enhancements helpful for your writing life.

Join me on a journey to creativity, a place where writers can frolic and play. Well, maybe not frolic and play, but certainly grow and prosper. Let my words be the battery which jumpstarts your own.

Mary Beth Magee
Poplarville, MS

Introduction

Each of us sees the world through a different lens. Your past experiences, education, personality and cultural background help to form the lens. As you deal with the world on a day-to-day basis, your perspective grows and changes. Your needs as a writer change. How do you meet those needs?

When you engage the tools of your mind and experiences to solve writing problems and inspire new works, you utilize creativity. In this book, you will see examples from many realms. After all, we write about what is, what was and what may come to be. We should take in information from everything and everywhere.

For example, a teacher puts together a lesson plan to involve students in the learning process. A businessman calculates a strategy for overcoming a supply chain problem. An inventor works on a new product to meet a societal need. A doctor works on a new treatment protocol for an illness. A writer seeks new plots and characters to entrance readers. Each of them puts creativity to work.

In this book, you will find suggestions, techniques and exercises to help you connect to your own creative well. I will also give you examples of some of the ways I keep my creativity flowing, in the hope those tips will help you find your own tools and processes.

Creativity easily could form the subject of a lifelong intellectual pursuit. A starting point for the first leg of the journey awaits you just ahead.

What is Creativity?

Ask any group of people to define creativity and you will probably get as many different answers as there are people in the group. Everyone seems to have a very personal idea about creativity. In its most strict definition, creativity is nothing more complicated than "the ability to create."[i] Scientists and behaviorists go a bit farther.

> "...creativity is a multidimensional domain that could be executed in the arts, science, stage performance, the commercial enterprise and business innovation (Sawyer, 2006). Following Baas et al. (2015) who defined the roots of creative cognition in the arts and sciences, creativity is not just a cultural or social construct. Instead, it is an essential psychological and cognitive process as well (Csikszentmihalyi, 1999; Sawyer, 2006; Kaufman, 2009; Gaut, 2010; Perlovsky and Levine, 2012)."[ii]

Take a handful of random ingredients from the refrigerator and pantry. Put them together in a scrumptious dish and serve it. The result comes from creativity at work. Great chefs use it all the time.

Look at a piece of fabric. Cut it out, sew it and embellish it. Wear the garment. Creativity strikes again, the same creativity used by the world's most famous designers.

Stand before a load which needs to be moved. Look at the equipment at hand. Put the pieces of equipment together in a combination to handle the load.

Study a task and choose the tools needed to complete it. Apply the tools to the project and enjoy the result.

Creativity has solved the problem. This aspect of problem-solving with creativity has taken humanity from caves to palaces.

So, why do we get so hung up on creativity?

Over the years, common usage of "creativity" has come to refer most often to the visual arts. Being creative has come to be synonymous with being artistic. If a person cannot draw or paint, they may be written off as "not creative." Not so. Creativity takes so many more forms than just the arts.

As writers, we must embrace creativity not only in the plots we imagine but also in the details of presenting those plots to our readers. The brilliant idea is not enough. We must write it in such a creative way that our reader can suspend disbelief (for a work of fiction) or follow the premise and learn from it.

I hope, as you go through this book, you will see the many ways creativity can be expressed, not only in your writing, but also in the practical world and in our minds. You will learn ways to nurture and use your own creativity to make the world a better place.

A Formula for Creativity

Creativity does not take place in a vacuum. I believe a distinct formula or recipe comes into play. Although the recipe is particular in its format, it is chaotic in its implementation. Start with the basic components and follow your own instincts and interests to complete the process.

INSPIRATION

+ IMAGINATION

+ INFORMATION

CREATIVITY

Put the ingredients of the recipe together and creativity happens. The proportions, like any good recipe, may vary. Ingredients may be added in any order. The result may take many different forms. Yet each will be a sample of creativity at work.

Take a look at each of these ingredients. See how they contribute to the finished product.

On Inspiration

Inspiration

Remember your last "Aha!" moment, the instant you saw a new path or identified the source of a problem? That instant marks inspiration at work. Think of inspiration as the heart of creativity.

Inspiration comes from within. Your heart, your mind, and your processing of the facts lead to inspiration. It comes from a place deep inside where all of the "stuff" you have taken into your brain gets whirled together like ingredients in a cerebral blender. What comes out is the ultimate creative smoothie!

Children are real pros at this process. Give them a big empty cardboard box, and they are inspired to become pirate captains or astronauts or part of a beleaguered garrison or…you get the idea. A blanket becomes a tent or a sail or a hero's cape. No rules, just fun.

Their inspiration comes from the supplies at hand. Rather than fret about what they do not have, they draw inspiration from what they do have.

We writers should seek to remain connected to the same childlike attitude which allows inspiration to flourish. Growing up does not mean we must lose the wonder of life.

Sources of Inspiration

For inspiration to work well, it has to be nourished. You can nourish your inspirational stockpile from a number of sources. Like tributaries feeding into a major river, these sources will help your inspiration flow ever stronger.

Collect things

Things which make you smile, make you happy, exercise your brain, and make you think all help to spark ideas, and make you want to keep going. The format may be a physical item, an image of an item or notes about an item. Collect them in whatever form works for you.

I happen to love books, flowers, all things nautical, puffins and zebras. So, I surround myself with the things which make me happy and bring a smile to my face. I collect photos of the things I love. I collect figurines and stuffed animals. I decorate with silk and living flowers. This bookshelf, just behind the desk in my office, brings me lots of inspiration each time I enter the room.

Some of the books in my collection are ones I have read and loved too much to let go. Some of the books talk about the things I love. Reference books in my collection help me grow in my craft. And some of the books, I am proud to say, are ones I have written or to which I have contributed.

If you have ever watched "The Ray Bradbury Theater" or visited the Center for Ray Bradbury Studies at Indiana University, you have seen one of my heroes as he worked when he was alive. Ray Bradbury's office held memorabilia and notes accumulated during his decades of living.[iii] Photos, statues, framed correspondence, miniatures, giant stuffed creatures, typewriters, awards and books, books, books! As he said in one version of the opening credits for his television series, he could not possibly go hungry for ideas in this environment.

You can create your own version of his motherlode of inspiration. Whether you display them on shelves or walls, file them in file cabinets or store them digitally, your treasures of life will help to feed your creative engine. Things you've achieved, things you hope to achieve, things you love – all contribute to inspiration.

Some industries call this dream building, a way to keep your goals and dreams firmly before you. Some label the process positive reinforcement. The label you hang on it is less important than accessing the process itself.

Collect memories of your successes, reminders of your goals and encouragement for the rough spots. And there will be rough spots, times when your brain is too tired to see the next step or a rejection letter stings like a snakebite. The recollections of successes will help you to recover from those stalls and keep going.

Another thought about encouragement: it can be *about* you or it can be something which speaks *to* you.

A note from a reader of "Well done! I loved the book," is encouragement about you. Keep those "Way to go!" notes for the days when you feel as though you have failed. They can remind you of the taste of success and keep you on track when a harsh editor or unkind review tries to scuttle your journey.

Outside encouragement may come from stories of overcomers, inspirational quotes or any other source where you can draw strength from another's success. Look at their pattern and adapt it to your own needs.

One of my "refuse to part with" books is a battered 1946 Readers Digest anthology I grew up with and inherited from my mother, entitled *Getting the Most Out of Life*. Cover to cover, it gives me hope and joy. I have read it multiple times over the years and will continue to read it as long as I am able.

I am a huge fan of the Chicken Soup for the Soul® series, too (even before I had the privilege of appearing in it). Such books remind me to keep going when my will flags.

Few climbers reach the summit of their target mountain without preparation, tools and a support team. Your collection contains all those elements for your inspiration. Even on those days when there is not anyone around to cheer you on, your collection will help.

Creativity 19

The view from the mountaintop of your creativity will take your breath away. Do not be afraid to make the climb. The reward is worth the effort.

List a few of the things you have collected which inspire you:

_____
_____
_____
_____
_____

Where do you keep or display them? How do they help you in your writing?

_____
_____
_____

Photograph places, people and things.

Whether you are talking about places you have been, people you have met, or things you have seen, take plenty of photographs along the way. Use those photographs to remind you of what you have achieved, what you want to achieve and what you are doing to achieve it.

This photo was one of many I took while on the Hattiesburg Daylily Driving Tour several years ago. Daylily breeders across the region, members of the Hattiesburg Area Daylily Society,[iv] open their gardens for public viewing over a spring weekend. We drove from one beautiful location to another during a full day of fellowship and flowers.

The picture, along with its companions and my memories of the day, became the inspiration for my first novel, *Death in the Daylilies*. The photographs became my reference materials as well as my inspiration. One of them even became the book's cover image.

A photo I took in Alaska surprised me when I had the pictures developed. (I took this with my trusty 35 mm, back in the days of film, before digital cameras and smart phones.)

We had taken a ride on The White Pass & Yukon Route Railroad, a scenic railway out of Skagway. Instead of just the few impressive boulders along a wild river gorge I hoped I had captured, I discovered I had a stunning image which included soaring mountains and towering trees. The photo never fails to transport me back to the narrow-gauge train ride and a delightful excursion along the Yukon River to the U.S.-Canada border. I treasure the photo and the memory of a trip with my family. It also inspires me to try to write books which will lift the hearts of readers the way the photo lifts my own heart.

One of my most cherished photos is one of Otto Penzler and me at a Killer Nashville conference. I have read Mr. Penzler's columns and essays for most of my life and meeting him was a thrill. The photo reminds me to aim high in my choice of those I look up to and say "Thank you" for their inspiration when I get the opportunity.

Want more photos to inspire you? Check out Caroline Topperman's book *Tell Me What You See*, a collection of photo prompts designed to bring out the story in you.

Image resources include unsplash.com, iStock by Getty Images, Shutterstock and other online image sources. Some require a purchase/license to use the photo; browsing for inspiration is free.

Think of photographs which inspire you. Do you see a pattern in them? Do any impact your writing life? Why?

_____
_____
_____
_____
_____

Copy things

This is a secret I learned from art students.

They copy the works of the great masters, not as an attempt to forge the work and fool someone, but as an exercise designed to help them understand the skills and techniques which go into creating a masterpiece. They learn image balance, develop an eye for detail and investigate a myriad of techniques.

Visit any art museum and you will likely see art students bent over their sketchbooks, learning by doing. "The practice of copying masterpieces has been one of the cornerstones of traditional art education for a long time."[v]

In 2015, the Rijksmuseum in Amsterdam in the Netherlands instituted a program called #startdrawing. As Wim Pijbes, the museum's general director, explains, "In our busy lives we don't always realize how beautiful something can be. We forget how to look really closely. Drawing helps because you see more when you draw. People who want to draw are always welcome in the Rijksmuseum."[vi]

I love the point about forgetting how to look closely. We, as writers, must look closely at the world around us and the topic of our work if we are to connect successfully with our readers.

My late paternal grandmother crocheted, and she crocheted beautifully. She could not follow a written pattern for anything, but she could look at someone else's finished piece and copy it to perfection. Once she figured out the stitch placement of a particular motif, she could branch out and use it to create her own patterns for everything from delicate doilies to lace collars for dresses and snuggly afghans. She copied to learn to create.

As a teenager, I fell in love with poetry. Since I could not afford to purchase copies of all of the books containing my favorites, I started collecting them in a spiral bound notebook, handwritten. As I copied those great poems over the years, I learned more about the rhythm of a poem, rhyme schemes, subjects and poetic forms. All of these elements demonstrated themselves in the notebook, courtesy of the great poets of the past. The poems I copied inspired me to learn more about writing poetry. When I write a poem today, I have all those poets of the past to thank for the lessons.

Sometimes, I write out a particularly beautiful or powerful prose passage from a book or article I am reading. This practice helps me get closer to the words, so I can better create my own passages with similar impact. The smooth coursing of a pen or pencil across paper reinforces the author's impact on me and activates my own creative thoughts. Learning and practicing the patterns of excellent phrases hones my own skills and inspires me. Keeping the copies of them close reminds me of the target of excellence those authors have set for me.

None of these copying techniques are meant to condone plagiarism or forgery, but rather to help school the learner in the tools of a discipline, in our case - writing. Always give proper credit to the works of others.

Copy the best of those who have achieved what you want to achieve, so you can learn from the steps to success they have laid out for you. You will nourish your creative soul with positive lessons.

Copying can also offer insights into the steps of a particular skill or craft. These perceptions can help to shape characters and plots, so do not limit yourself to copying written works. Remain open to opportunities to copy excellence in any medium.

What are some of the works which you can copy as a learning tool?

_____
_____
_____
_____
_____

Study things

No one of us knows everything there is to know. By employing lifelong study, you not only feed your creativity, you also keep yourself young.

As a writer, I study writing techniques, genre descriptions, specific topics which apply to my books, psychology, criminology and more. I read the books of writers I admire and analyze why I admire them. If an opportunity to attend a webinar pops up when I am available, I grab it.

For *Death in the Daylilies*, I studied daylily growers and their techniques, the propagation methods applicable to daylilies, and other aspects of the culture. I talked with growers and breeders. I even bought a few cultivars for myself. I did not know much about them when I started, but I learned. The more I learned, the more I appreciated those who grow these beautiful flowers and the more their work inspired me.

I knew my research had paid off when a professional daylily breeder recommended the book to his peers, saying "She got it right." His comment meant the world to me.

We are told "Write what you know." The warning implicit in the instruction is "Don't try to fake it. You'll be found out." What the statement does not mention is how long you have to have known your subject. The secret is, not always a long time if you probe the subject in-depth and do not write beyond your knowledge level.

Studying a new topic can energize your creativity. Learning invigorates the mind which in turn feeds inspiration. You do not require a college degree to know a subject well enough to use it in your writing.

Not sure what you would like to study? Walk the stacks in your local library. Scan magazines and newspapers. Look at college catalogs. Visit websites like Atlas Obscura (https://www.atlasobscura.com/) for a variety of offbeat topics to pique your interest. The site boasts information on over 20,000 unusual places, as well as oddities of nature.

What fields of interest would you like to study?

_____
_____
_____
_____

Where will you go to study them?

_____
_____
_____
_____

Listen to inspiring music

What sort of music lifts you? Is it a single musical form or a variety of them? Listen to those pieces which make you feel empowered, uplifted, filled with joy. The ones which fill your head with images as you listen with your eyes closed.

When I was a teenager, some of the people I knew would collect a hand-selected group of recordings onto a cassette and call it a "mix tape." Nowadays, people set up a playlist on an electronic device. The medium has changed but the idea is the same: listen to the music you love. The name of the method is less important than the musical choices. Set up your own playlist of music which motivates, inspires and invigorates you.

Do not let anyone tell you what you *must* listen to for inspiration. Choose the music which inspires you, regardless of the format. My own list includes selections from classical, gospel, traditional jazz, show tunes, soul, rock and roll and country. Some come with lyrics while others are instrumentals. Some make me laugh. Some make me cry. Some make me cheer. Each of them speaks to me in its own way. Each of them offers me a mental or emotional boost.

Sometimes I have music playing in the background for company as I write. Sometimes

I have it blasting when I need a boost of ideas and I let myself be carried away by the beat. I reach for music as precisely as a doctor writes a prescription, playing the musical medicine I need as I work. Different tracks for different situations, but all effective for me.

The most important feature of your choices should be how they make you feel. My favorites may not help you at all and your favorites may not work for me. No problem. Your choices are right for you and nothing else matters.

What type of music do you turn to for writing help? What form of music lifts you and inspires you? List some of your favorites here.

_____
_____
_____
_____
_____

On Imagination

Imagination

Imagination, coming up with new ideas, forms the backbone of creativity. Envision a new way to approach a problem by bringing previous knowledge together in a new way and you have called on your imagination.

As a society, we value imagination. We celebrate "imaginative" productions and solutions. When technology and imagination meet, we applaud "imagineering," a word coined by Alcoa Aluminum and trademarked by Walt Disney Corporation.[vii] Your own imagination is every bit as valuable.

Where do we get the imaginative ideas from which we can create? Curiosity is key. A sense of "I wonder about…" something, a desire to know a little more about a topic or situation starts the process. The same curiosity behind the popularity of "reality" programming or the desire to head toward a siren pushes imagination and, in turn, creativity.

Who, what, where, when, how and why questions can provide powerful factual insights. Imagination takes over from there.

Begin by letting your thoughts run in a multitude of directions from the task at hand. Call it brainstorming, thought mapping or any other label you choose. Let ideas and images come, and then build on them.

Once more, take a look at children. I see this creative brainstorming demonstrated very clearly when I participate in a children's library program. We start out with a simple idea, like a figure made from toilet paper rolls covered in aluminum foil or construction paper. By the end of the session, we end up with an incredible variety of creations, all sprung from the minds of the participating children. Robots, doctors, dolls and more appear from the fertile fields of juvenile imaginations watered with an array of supplies.

In workshops with puppeteer Laura Anne Ewald of The Everyman Puppet Theatre,[viii] I have watched a single sheet of paper or a paper plate transform into fanciful puppets of intricate design. Children use nothing more than paper, glue and crayons or markers to bring their creations to life.

The children are not hindered by what is expected or what reality says. They cut loose with a big dose of "What can I make from this stuff?" Imagination, fueled by whatever supplies are at hand, burns brightly to light the way to creative play.

Here are some ways to power up your imagination, but do not feel limited to these.

Add whatever methods you have found work for you from past experience. Glean ideas from others, as well. As a group of individuals pooling our strengths, we have far more resources than any one person alone.

Read

Read everything you can get your hands on which interests you or catches your eye. You never know what will spark your imagination. Fiction or nonfiction, historical or contemporary, book or periodical, any genre at all will offer fuel to your imagination's engine.

While researching the nearby Pearl River for a story point, I stumbled across an online article about the identification of a new species of turtle in the area. The article gave me the basis for a series of children's books. "Pearl the Turtle" was inspired by *Graptemys pearlensis*, the Pearl River map turtle, an endangered species indigenous to the Pearl River and its tributaries in Mississippi and Louisiana. The first story, *Pearl's Pool*, dealt with peer pressure, thinking for yourself and knowing when you have all you need.

Pearl's *persona* later came together with a situation I encountered on a quiet country road. I spotted a box turtle poised on the edge of the road as though about to cross. I stopped my car and moved the beautiful amphibian to the other side of the road in an attempt to prevent it from being run over by an inattentive driver.

The two turtles meet in the second Pearl the Turtle book, *Pearl Makes a Friend,* and explore the idea of becoming friends with someone who does not look like you. Even plush turtles can use new friends.

Neither of these books, nor the others in the works would have come about if I hadn't taken the time to read the article mentioning the newly identified species.

Part of your mental exercise to prepare for writing should be to read. Check the headlines on the newspaper or a news website. Read a chapter or two in a novel or a nonfiction book. Peruse an article or two in a magazine. Whether you are researching a topic or just reading for general information, read.

When you take in information on a wide array of topics from a variety of sources, your mind can start to process the data in new ways. Like some sort of buffet restaurant menu, your brain can take a little something from one tray, something from a second bin and top it with a big scoop of something from another display. You have prepared a meal to feed your imagination and it will respond with a banquet of ideas.

Read in your own genre(s), read in other genres, read news magazines and websites, but read something every day. Your knowledge, your imagination and your skills will grow.

Where do you find assorted information to read? What sort of information sources appeal to you?

_____

_____

_____

_____

Visit

Get out of your everyday space. Visit a place you have not been before, maybe normally would not have even thought of going. I always find museums geared to children get my imagination going. Kids tend to look at the world through a lens of "everything is possible." When you spend time around them in a rich environment, you will start looking at things in the same way.

How about a historic or nature site in your area which you have skipped in the past? Those docents can fill your head with fascinating tidbits on the subject to spark your imagination. Some obscure detail can be just the prompt you need to get your ideas working.

Old solutions can be adapted and updated to address current writing situations. Ideas from the past can lead the way to newer ideas and innovations in your works. A bit of local history can be just the color to bring your story to life.

I love hanging out in nature preserves and arboretums. While walking a trail through The Crosby Arboretum in Picayune, MS, I was struck by how isolated some areas were. A crime could take place there unwitnessed! And so was born *Ambush at the Arboretum*, my second novel.

Another location I visited in the past and plan to use is the Tea Tasting Room at JD Farms[ix]. The blueberry and tea farm just outside of town offers tea tasting in a dining room-like setting which set me to imagining a formal tea party showdown *a la* Agatha Christie for my current work-in-progress, *Blood on the Bottletree*.

The setting, rich in the charm of a variety of tea services and the aromas of tea blends, speaks to me of intrigue and tradition, perfect for a tasteful showdown. And who knew Mississippi could grow tea?

Something as simple as a restaurant or coffeehouse can get the creative juices flowing. Listen to the conversations of fellow diners (discreetly, of course) and make notes of interesting comments, descriptions, names or anything else which captures your attention. Once the information percolates through your own worldview, you will have all sorts of imaginative ways to go.

List some places you would like to visit for inspiration:

_____
_____
_____
_____
_____

Attend

Look for cultural and educational events to attend. Your public library or community college probably holds lectures on topics which interest you. The cost will be reasonable (maybe even free) and the rewards great. Events about arts, science and history can lead to ideas in other realms and *vice versa*, so do not discount any intriguing topic.

Visit collections such as natural history museums, historic sites, reconstructed locales, vocational history museums and even oddball places.

This bizarre creature, a combination of alligator and carousel pony, is part of the Abita Mystery House,[x] (also known as the UCM Museum) in Abita Springs, LA. An eclectic folk art museum, the Mystery House offers many strange "artifacts," including a huge collection of paint-by-number works, craft stick sculptures and other amazing oddities. Your imagination cannot help but feed on the outlandish exhibits there.

Another such delight exists in Hattiesburg, MS as Hattiesburg Pocket Museum.[xi] Hidden down a side alley in the downtown area, the museum brings in unusual displays of a plethora of subjects. The exhibits change on a regular basis, offering a continually fresh source for fueling the imagination.

Take advantage of writing events whenever you can. Attend anything, from clubs to conferences, lectures and open mike nights to one-author readings. All it takes is one good idea to make your attendance worthwhile. Chances are good you will find more than one. You will gather information on your craft and recharge your creative battery. Some seemingly minor fact or off-hand comment might be the spark which sends your imagination into overdrive.

Meet with others who share your interests outside of writing. You can share insights to help each other grow.

List any events or locations that you would like to attend:

_____
_____
_____
_____

Borrow Ideas from the Arts

Learning about other expressive media can help your own expressive work improve. Art forms can feed on each other.

Ekphrastic poetry is a form which yields a poem based on a physical work of art. The original work may be a painting or sculpture, some sort of needlework or other visual art. The poet expresses in words the feelings triggered by the artwork.

Writing competitions often ask for stories based on or inspired by a particular image. Artists create images which depict a particular scene in a story. A song inspires a movie script. A book sparks an image for a painter. The circle goes on as the arts intertwine to strengthen each other.

Take time to view artworks in person, in books or online. Note your reaction to the work and any ideas generated by what you are viewing. Remember, this is not about becoming an art critic. Respond with whatever you feel as you take in the particular piece.

Consider blocking out part of the image with your hand or a piece of paper or zooming in if you are viewing it on screen. How does the change of view impact your impression of the work? What ideas does the new view give you?

What details do you notice which you had missed previously?

You do not have to be an arts writer to try this creative exercise. Write a brief impression of this piece of sculpture.

Poetry or prose, fact or fiction, your choice. What do you see, feel or think when you look at Antoine Bourdelle's sculpture Hercules the Archer?[xii]

Imagine yourself meeting this fellow at a sporting event, encountering him on a hunt, being introduced at a party. Let the thoughts and ideas flow freely. Whether you approach your piece as an interview, a product ad, a fictional story or something else altogether, you will find your creativity firing on all pistons.

I took this photograph of the statue in the Sydney and Walda Besthoff Sculpture Garden at the New Orleans Museum of Art in City Park, New Orleans, LA. The statue formerly stood in front of the museum and was always one of my favorite landmarks when I was a child. Now it shares a vast area with a delightful collection of other sculptures in the park, outdoors just beyond the museum building. A visit to the garden allows one to enjoy nature and art at the same time.

Just as photographs can prompt fresh ideas, so can works of art in all media. Enjoy them through visits or art books. Whatever your taste in art, you are sure to find works to delight you.

List some pieces of art (in any media) which spark your imagination:

_____

_____

_____

_____

List potential resources for viewing art in your area.

_____

_____

Observe

Pay attention to what is going on around you. Look with a dedicated eye to pull in the details, large and small, which can help you fuel your imagination.

The human brain seems to be hardwired to look for patterns and connections[xiii] in the world around us. The details we perceive can contribute to our pattern recognition, but we have to make the effort to be aware of the details. Once we perceive the stimulus of a particular shape, sound or aroma, our creative mind will make associations and spark ideas.

When was the last time you watched the clouds with an eye toward something other than the weather? There are rich fields for imagination, ready for harvest, in the ever-

shifting shapes and shadows of the clouds. For instance, what do you see in this cloud photo?

Give yourself a chance to really look skyward sometime soon. You may find fanciful creatures, historical figures, impressive buildings or more. And everything you see is stoking your imagination. Far from wasting time, cloud watching is an imagination-building activity.

Mississippi even has its own version of the Grand Canyon[xiv]. Red Bluff, located near Foxworth, MS offers spectacular views of nature and its power. Take advantage of such natural occurrences and let them power your writing engine.

Observe with all your senses. Each sense sets the stage for your perception of the world. When you employ them to gather the details of your surroundings, you give your imagination free rein.

Here is an exercise on using your senses. Close your eyes to avoid distraction by what you see. Concentrate on your surroundings. You may want to have someone read the questions to you one by one to allow you to respond without interruption.

> a. What do you hear? Is it what you expected to hear? If not, what expected sound or sounds are absent? What unexpected sounds are present? What do they tell you about your environment?
>
> b. What do you feel? Is the air cool or warm? Is the air moving around you or still? Do you sense dampness or dryness?
>
> c. What do you smell? Scientists tell us a sense of smell is closely linked to our memory and emotions.[xv] What aromas do you identify in your current environment? What do they say to you? What feelings and thoughts do they kindle?
>
> d. What do you taste?[xvi] Inhale through your opened mouth and concentrate on the sensations you feel on your tongue. Are they pleasant or unpleasant? How do you feel about the taste? What does it bring to mind?
>
> e. Now open your eyes. What do you see? Did your senses prepare you for what you are viewing or was there a surprise? Do you notice something you had previously overlooked? How do you feel about the outcome?

Make notes about the senses you experienced. How do they help you to understand the world around you? How can you use them to enhance your creativity and apply them to your current situation?

All of our senses play into our perception of the world and our interactions with it. There is a reason why grocery stores send the aroma of freshly baked bread out into the store, why advertisers choose particular colors, why call systems choose particular "wait" music.

When we tune into our sensory input, we turn on new possibilities for solving our problem, answering our question, or revitalizing our creativity. List some interesting things you have observed which got your imagination operating:

_____
_____
_____
_____

Play

Play allows us to explore possibilities without boundaries. I am talking about logic games, puzzles, word games, jigsaw puzzles, role playing games and such. The time you spend playing games can refresh your mind and in turn, your creativity.[xvii]

One game, guaranteed to provoke fun and imagination, is creating crazy acronyms. Start with the letters and create the title to go along. Pick a word, any word, and run with it. (Admit it, you have wondered about all those governmental agency and project acronyms, haven't you? Which came first, the name or the acronym?)

Many years ago, I belonged to a local writers group focused on writing science fiction. The official name of the group began as the South Mississippi Professional Science Fiction Writers Association. The pretentious and overly long moniker did not last.

One of the members suggested we just call ourselves "SMART" because we were all intelligent enough to appreciate science fiction. A little pompous in its humor, perhaps, but it paved the way to what eventually became our permanent name – South Mississippi Armadillo Racing Team. A definite case of creating a name to fit the letters.

The fanciful title lent itself to all sorts of imaginative scenarios. Were we humans who raced armadillos? Armadillos who drove race cars? Race car drivers who kept armadillos as pets? Were the race cars powered by armadillos in the engine? Was the racing taking place on Earth or somewhere else? We had a great deal of fun with the crazy ideas generated.

Perhaps you can even guess <u>my</u> favorite description: we were writers with tough enough shells to ward off rejection letters and negative reviews, and we could roll up in our shells to roll up to our typewriters (I know, I am dating myself here) to tell our stories.

All the descriptions are fanciful and fun. We had a blast with our name. Some of us even went so far as to acquire armadillo gear to celebrate our group. The game gave us joy.

Another form of play comes from crafts. Whether you prefer simple crafts such as adult coloring books or more detailed forms such as model building, needlework, jewelry making or cake decorating, working in a beloved craft can deliver relaxation and mental refreshment. Take advantage of the opportunity.

Play can take many forms. Physical play, a rousing game of your favorite sport, can go a long way to rejuvenate your creativity. The increased blood flow and endorphin production will help you physically and mentally.

My granddaughter (who is six years old as I write this) and I play hide-and-seek regularly. She lives 900 miles away, so we play virtually. She moves off screen while I count, then I start my seeking.

"I wonder if she went into the garage." I tap-tap-tap on the desktop as I "walk" to the garage. And on I go, tapping my way through the rooms of the house: laundry room, upstairs to the bedrooms, down to the basement playroom, back up to the living room, into the kitchen, over to the patio door to check the backyard, and so on.

She giggles hysterically as I miss my guess, then pops back into view when I "find" her in her chosen hiding place. She gets to imagine me walking through her house, I get to imagine where she might have chosen to hide this time and we have a great time. Distance may separate us, but imagination brings us together through the medium of play.

Scientists are digging deeper into the role of play in wellbeing.[xviii] Even a rousing game of Solitaire can let your mind work on a different level than usual and free your creative thoughts. By changing mental gears for a little while, you give yourself a chance to see the world from a fresh perspective.

Whether you play alone or with others, take time to play. Your mind will thank you and your writing will flourish.

What games and/or sports do you play for mental refreshment and imagination building?

_____

_____

_____

_____

_____

"What If?" the Situation

Long a tool of speculative fiction authors, "What if?" offers limitless ways for your imagination to bloom. From alien worlds across the universe to alternative history here on earth, "What if?" can change a writer's perspective. The same question can help in whatever situation you are facing, as the 2020 COVID-19 pandemic proved.

Just take a look at these examples. What if…

- Teachers made the switch to video classes online?
- Public libraries began offering children's story time sessions online?
- Churches offered video services through social media?
- Garment companies began manufacturing masks and medical gowns instead of fashionable attire?
- Breweries and distilleries bottled hand sanitizer instead of alcoholic beverages?
- Restaurants and stores offered curbside pickup when patrons could not come inside?
- Musicians played concerts through video sharing applications or performed in small groups from balconies or rooftops?

- Rival drug companies joined forces to increase vaccine production?

Those businesses and services and many more used the "what if" scenario to find ways to keep going. Check out YouTube for additional examples of how people coped with the changes brought about by this horrible pandemic.

Maybe you are facing a plot problem, or you cannot come up with a hook for your next article. Instead of "I can't do *whatever it is*," start with "What if I can?" From there, go on to "what if?" your way to possible solutions to help you get back to your writing. Here are a few examples:

- a.) **What if** the setting changed? Move a Western to a South Pacific island, an urban story to a farm, for example.
- b.) **What if** the time period changed? Writer Arthur Laurents took Shakespeare's *Romeo and Juliet* into the twentieth century and created the book which eventually became the hit musical *West Side Story*.
- c.) **What if** the characters' roles swapped? When a parent and child trade places, members of different ethnic groups trade races, or a hero becomes a villain magic can occur. Perspectives and behaviors may undergo dramatic revisions, leading

to fresh insights for you and your characters. Even if you stay with the original storyline, you will stay there with additional ideas.

d.) What if the characters' names changed? Would Pearl Pureheart have been perceived in the same way if her name had been Stella Slimebucket? What if James Bond had been named Walter Smith? How do names shape lives? How about if the name includes a title of some kind?

e.) What if the characters' gender changed? For example, does a man approach the world from the same POV as a woman? How would your story change if your main characters changed gender? What strategic adjustments might your character make?

f.) What if your research takes you in a new direction? Review your research, looking for tidbits you might have missed. Your reevaluation of the information can provide "Ah-ha!" moments of crisis creation and plot solution. I found the motive for the crime in *Death in the Daylilies* hidden in my research.

g.) What if you were writing the same story in a different genre? How would the story change? How would the conventions of the new genre impact the work?

h.) What if no dialog was allowed? How would your scenes change?

i.) What if <u>only</u> dialog was allowed?

Do not be afraid to pummel whatever your current problem is with as many "What if" questions as it takes to get past the feeling of "I can't" and move on to "I can." You will find "What if" questions to be one of the most creative tools in your imagination's toolbox. Take them out on a regular basis and put them to use.

List some "What If" questions to help your problem-solving for your current project:

_____
_____
_____
_____
_____

Beyond "What If?"

Other aspects of challenging yourself with your current work can offer new insights and ideas to move you forward to your best work.

1. Change the Point of View
   Answer questions about a situation from several POVs to get a fresh understanding. Look at the event as:
   a.) You, as the person living the incident (I did this.)
   b.) You, the person affected by the incident (This was done to me.)
   c.) You, the neutral person observing the incident (I see someone doing this)

   The multiple POV technique has been used by authors like Anne McCaffrey in her Chronicles of Pern books and stories. She tells the history of Pern from the perspective of the dragonriders (the defenders of Pern), the Harper Hall (the record keepers and teachers of Pern) and other members of the society. Each main character brings his or her own observations, experiences and opinions to the table. Rather than repetitious, her novels have a sense of "Now I understand more clearly."

A similar technique was used in the animated film "Hoodwinked," telling the story of Little Red Riding Hood from each participant's POV with hilarious results.

I am not advocating "head hopping," which can leave your reader lost and confused. This is a planned approach which gives different viewpoints an opportunity to be heard. To write it well takes work. To play with it for inspiration is much easier.

Just as you can choose to tell the story from different viewpoints, we can use different perspectives to reveal different aspects of an event. You may not use all of the perspectives in your work, but you'll gain fresh insights.

2. Role Reversal
   Can the streetwise kid grow up to be a straight-as-an-arrow cop instead of a hoodlum? Suppose the privileged debutante chooses to dedicate her life to helping the underprivileged? What happens if the faithful family pet becomes a deranged killer? How does a self-centered loner become a rescuer?

Anytime you flip the reader's presumptions, you open your story up to fresh action. Do not be afraid to explore a role reversal, even if you do not use your discoveries in this particular work.

While related to role swapping, role reversal works for a single character rather than requiring a pair of them.

3. Rags to Riches to Rags
Change your protagonist's fortunes for a moment. Let the poor become rich. Make the rich become poor.

How do these changes reveal underlying truths about personality and true character? What can you learn about your main players? Do these insights give you creative fodder?

Laugh often.

The Biblical prescription for laughter (Proverbs 17:22) still holds. Psychologists examine the link between creativity and laughter as a common theme. While enhancing creativity does not require you to become a stand-up comic, understanding how those presenters work can help you take the next step toward sparks and fireworks of your own.

> "Surprise is at the heart of comedy. Surprise is also at the heart of *creativity*. Creativity is about more than just producing something. It's about producing something in a new way, a different way, a surprising way. So, if you want to be creative in your life or work, it's important to be available to surprise."[xix]

One handy tool is a laughter journal. Keep notes about events and situations which made you laugh. Review those entries when you feel stuck in a rut. They can help kick you into gear.[xx] Whether a joke, a silly mishap or a serendipitous event, a revisited laugh can bring you out of the doldrums.

Remember the alligator-carousel horse sculpture you saw earlier? Off-beat folk art museums like the Abita Mystery House serve up laughter in big quantities, so indulge your appetite for joy often.

How does humor help? There are several channels at work. The distraction from thinking about a problem, relaxing for a moment, stretching your creative muscles—all of these and more are ways humor stimulates creativity.[xxi]

Just as play can help free you from the everyday routine, so can humor. From the corniest "Knock, Knock" joke to the most sophisticated comedy routine, laughter is beneficial to your creative flow. Take a moment for a smile just for you on the next page.

> Knock, Knock
> *(Who's there)*
> Plum
> *(Plum who?)*
> Plum' brilliant, that's you!

List some things which make you laugh:

_____
_____
_____
_____
_____

On Information

Information

If Inspiration is the heart of creativity and Imagination is its backbone, Information provides the brains. Without information to guide us, we would flounder as we tried to create.

We have already discussed the importance of taking in information from a variety of sources as it pertains to inspiration and imagination. Take a more in-depth look now at the basic process of garnering and using information.

Reading

Today's researchers have more options than ever for accessing books. First and foremost, support your local library. Free access to books, past and present, helps to keep a society educated and informed and libraries are our first line of access without regard to income.

Print media, electronic formats and audio books offer access to fit a variety of lifestyles. Most modern works come in multiple formats. Choose the one which works best for your situation.

Many other book resources are free; some are minimal cost. Check out some of these sources for older material. If you are researching the writings, science or culture of a past era, you will enjoy these sites, which provide access to out-of-print and public domain materials.

a) Project Gutenberg (https://www.gutenberg.org/). As of this writing, Project Gutenberg boasts more than free 60,000 titles. These are out-of-print books available in .pdf format. You can read them on the site. Some can be download (often in a choice of electronic reader formats) to read later.

b) Open Library (https://openlibrary.org/) Open Library claims to have more than three million titles available. One of those titles is my old friend, *Getting the Most out of Life*! (https://openlibrary.org/works/OL15160539W/Getting_the_most_out_of_life?edition=gettingmostoutof00plea)

c) Many Books (https://manybooks.net/). More than 50,000 titles.

d) International Children's Digital Library (http://en.childrenslibrary.org/). This site focuses on books for young readers in a variety of languages.

For more sites which share ebooks, search the internet for "free ebook." Before you click any links to sites, be sure to open a separate tab and check for reviews of the site to help avoid spam or hazardous sites.

Audio books provide recorded versions of books for consumer listening. Some books are abridged, some unabridged. Audio books allow "reading" while you are engaged in some other activity.

Along the same vein as audio books, podcasts offer information on nearly any available topic to listeners via the internet. Search for podcasts on your subjects of interest and you can find programs to listen to while you exercise, work in the yard, commute or any other similar activity.

List your favorite resources for reading material:

_____
_____
_____
_____

Experience your world

We have talked about visiting various locales as learning experiences, but do not forget to just take time to experience whatever is around you *right now*. From relationships to nature, emotions to physical events, your world will stimulate your imagination with input. The world you inhabit will inspire you with opportunities to grow and challenges to meet.

Let the everyday become special and the unusual become celebratory. For example, I am accustomed to anoles and geckos running around the porch, but the day I found my own little "dinosaur" is one I treasure. The magnificent fence swift was more than happy to pose for me and waited until I could get my cell phone out of my pocket. I consider such an event to be a serendipitous gift.

Sit quietly with a cup of coffee or a glass of tea and soak in the nature around you. The relaxing buzz of a bee, the hypnotic zooming of a hummingbird, the lyrical song of a mockingbird can easily be missed if you do not listen for them. The heady aroma of nearby blooming flowers, the dappled pattern of sunlight through trees and the busy path of an anole on the prowl can escape notice. Take time to observe, enjoy and be renewed by nature around you.

Look at the world from a perspective of "What new and wonderful thing will happen next?" and you will find special experiences all around you. Take a moment to appreciate them. Keep a record them for future enjoyment.

List some serendipitous moments in your life:

_____

_____
_____
_____
_____

What can you do to experience more of them?

_____
_____
_____
_____
_____

Write it down

A journal or online note system can help you to organize all the pieces of information you have learned. Review your notes from time to time to give your brain the opportunity to integrate the ideas you have gleaned. Your subconscious can add the information to the store of knowledge at your disposal.

Have you seen the movie "Working Girl" with Harrison Ford and Melanie Griffith? When Griffith's character is challenged to explain how she came up with a particular business strategy, she pulls a conglomeration of seemingly unconnected articles and notes from her folder to show her process and prove she was the originator of the plan. Creativity at work!

The synthesis of information into inspiration through imagination requires some work on your part. If the information simply passes through your consciousness without making any impression, you will likely miss out on creative opportunities. Take the time to let it make an impression.

Examine each source like a rare jewel. Hold it up to the light of your perception, turn it to see how the light strikes from different directions. Ask yourself, "How can I apply this to my book (or my problem)?" The more attentive time you spend with the information, the greater potential impact it can have.

If the source material is your own, use it as a repository for comments, questions and references. Highlighters and pens make great companions to your own books and notebooks.

If you do not own the source material, then make notes about the information. A three-ring binder, a journal, a spiral bound notebook or computerized word processing program can help you take and keep notes in an orderly manner. Be sure to document the original source so you can find it again if needed.

If you found the information online, be sure to record the web address for future reference. Try printing the page or saving as a .pdf for your records. While not every webpage allows for such use, many do.

Where do you keep records of inspirational and imaginative information?

_____
_____
_____
_____
_____

Record your idea fragments

Do not lose the benefit of your creativity. When the idea strikes, jot it down along with any relevant details. Be prepared for those odd moments of inspiration.

Here are a few tools to help:
a.) a small notebook and pen or pencil near your bed,
b.) a notes app or voice recording app on your mobile device,
c.) a washable grease pencil in the shower,
d.) an erasable whiteboard.

These temporary storage methods represent only a handful of the ways you can capture your ideas in the moment for later reference and preservation. Find the way or ways which work best for you and use them regularly.

At the earliest opportunity, transfer the idea to a more permanent storage method. Flesh out any additional details you have come up with and keep adding to the record over time until you are ready to implement the idea.

An idea allowed to escape is no use to you. An idea savored and saved can grow into creative solutions.

Where do you save your idea fragments? How do you preserve them for future reference?

_____

_____

_____

_____

_____

Start Creating

A few last thoughts:

The well of creative thought refreshes the writer's mind. Visit it often to fill your bucket.

The preferred diet of creative thought is ideas. Feed your creativity frequently.

Creative thought flies free and knows no limits. Do not clip its wings.

Look into a mirror. Peering back at you is a creative mind, whether you realize it or not.

My hope for you and your visit to this book is you *will* realize the creative potential you have inside and give it a chance to bloom. Your writing and your life will change for the better.

Creativity becomes a lifelong process of seeing possibilities and exploring avenues. Do not limit yourself to one approach. Be open to all the options ahead.

Go forth and be creative!

Appendix

The Creativity Bill of Rights

1. *You have the God-given right to be creative.*
2. *You have the right to nurture your creativity.*
3. *You have the right to apply your creativity to a variety of situations and circumstances.*
4. *You have the right to appreciate the creative results of others.*
5. *You have the right to use curiosity as a divining rod to lead you toward creative discoveries in all realms of life.*
6. *You have the right to express your creativity in safe and productive ways*

which do no harm to others.

7. *You have the right to use your creativity to make your life, your family, your work, your community, and your world a better place.*

© Mary Beth Magee

A Few Suggested Games

- Word games such as Scrabble, anagrams, crossword puzzles
- Categories
- Rebus puzzles
- Sudoku puzzles
- Trivia games
- Jigsaw puzzles
- Problem-solving games such as mazes and matching games
- Role-playing games
- Rory's Story Cubes

Whether played online, in books or on tabletop boards, such games can enhance creativity.

Creativity Exercises

Here are a few exercises to get you started. Do not be afraid to create your own situations to continue.

- Imagine two historic characters from different eras, locations, or perspectives. For example, put Napoleon and Genghis Khan, Mother Teresa and Mao Zedong or Vincent Van Gogh and Albert Einstein in the same room. How would they interact? What would they talk about?
- Put a historic figure in a contemporary environment. How might he or she react? What questions would arise? What might seem unbelievable and what might seem a natural progression?
- Put a contemporary figure in a historic environment. What would the person miss most? What would be most appreciated about the period?
- Compare children's toys from the 1800s, 1900s and 2000s. What aspects have changed? What has remained the same?
- Examine the differences in food preparation between today and 200 years ago. What is better or healthier? What is less healthy or more difficult?
- What would happen if modern appliances stopped working? How would you cope with everyday tasks?
- Imagine yourself dropped in a foreign land. You have no local currency, you do not

speak the language, you do not know the customs. What would you do to fit in? Would you ask for help or try to hide your vulnerability? Why?

Some Suggested Reading

These are a few of the sources I turn to for encouragement and inspiration. Begin your own list and collection to keep you going.

Getting the Most out of Life: A Readers Digest Anthology

The Greatest Salesman in the World by Og Mandino

Chicken Soup for the Soul® series

The Places You'll Go by Dr. Seuss

The Power of Story series by Laura Anne Ewald

On Writing: A Memoir of the Craft by Stephen King

Tell Me What You See by Caroline Topperman

Storytime Crafts, Games and Gifts Using Recycled and Inexpensive Items by Mary Beth Magee

Atlas Obscura (https://www.atlasobscura.com/)

What other books or sources come to mind?

_____
_____
_____
_____

To Hercules

(On Antoine Bourdelle's *Hercules the Archer*)
by Mary Beth Magee

Noble sir, you've lost your garments.
Has your prey so stripped your pride?
Break your hunter's concentration
Long enough to go inside.

Put on trousers or a tunic,
Celtic kilt or Roman mail –
Anything, I beg you, archer,
For your undress leaves me pale.

Draw your bow in preparation,
Aim it high and set it loose.
Exact revenge against the thief
Who has exposed your bronze caboose.

Such disdain for social mores
May result in banishment.
Save your yourself by donning clothing,
Or stay hidden in your tent.

Hercules, I bow in wonder
At your muscles, strong and taut.
Now put your clothes on rippled sinew
Before a nasty cold you've caught.

© Mary Beth Magee

Photo Credits

Eat the Rainbow: Rezel Apacianado*

Sewing: Marília Castelli*

Tools: Jesse Orrico*

Bookshelf: Mary Beth Magee

Man with Red Backpack: Lucas Clara*

Daylily Garden: Mary Beth Magee

Alaska Landscape: Mary Beth Magee

Student: Santi Vedri*

Blanket Tent: Nathan Dumlao*

Pearl River Map Turtle: U.S. Geological Survey

Pearl and Becky: Mary Beth Magee

Arboretum Trail: Mary Beth Magee

Pouring Tea: Barrett Baxter*

Hercules the Archer Sculpture: Mary Beth Magee

Gray Chick Cloud: Mary Beth Magee

Red Bluff Canyon: Mary Beth Magee

Boxer with Punching Bag: Lorenzo Fattò Offidani*

Neon Laugh: Tim Mossholder*

Fence Swift Dragon: Mary Beth Magee

* Photos courtesy www.unsplash.com

Books by Mary Beth Magee

Fiction

The (LOL)^4 Mysteries
- Death in the Daylilies: Volume 1
- Ambush at the Arboretum: Volume 2

The Cypress Point Chronicles
- Volume 1: Cypress Point Confidences
- Volume 2: A Cypress Point Christmas
- Volume 3: Cypress Point Spirit

Journals

- Devotions from the Road of Life Journal: A Caregiver's Medical Log
- Getting Started in Your Own Kitchen: A Kitchen Planner and Cooking Journal for New Cooks
- The Rose of Friendship: A Gratitude Journal
- Get Started with Your Memoirs
- The Storyteller's Journal
- Sixty Days to Greater Writing Creativity

Nonfiction

Devotions from the Road of Life
- Volume 1: Hitting the Road
- Volume 2: Devotions for Caregivers
- Volume 3: When the Road Gets Rough

- Creativity: An Essential Tool for the Real World
- Jumpstart the Creativity in Your Writing
- Storytime Crafts, Games and Gifts Using Recycled and Inexpensive Items

Books for Children
- Grandpa's Mustache
- Pearl's Pool: Volume 1 of Pearl the Turtle
- Pearl Makes a Friend: Volume 2 of Pearl the Turtle
- Some More Cows
- The Promise Wreath

Poetry
- Songs of Childhood, Echoes of Years
- Life and All: The Journey

Anthology Appearances
Chicken Soup for the Soul®: Thanks to My Mom
Chicken Soup for the Soul®: The Spirit of America
Chicken Soup for the Soul®: Believe in Miracles
Treasures Found in a Cedar Chest
Celebrating Mississippi (Mississippi Poetry Society South Branch)
Mississippi Poetry Journal 2018 Contest Edition
Southern Holidays (Mississippi Poetry Society South Branch)

Maps of the Heart
Inspire Promise
Inspire Hope
Not Your Mother's Book on Being a Parent
Not Your Mother's Book on Being a Stupid Kid

Connect with Mary Beth Magee

Website: www.LOL4.net

Email: info@botr.com

Facebook: MaryBethMageeWrites

Twitter: MaryBethWrites

Etsy: https://www.etsy.com/shop/BOTRPress/

Café Press: http://www.cafepress.com/profile/121587126

Where to Find Books by Mary Beth Magee

Order through your local bookstore (they can order it if they do not currently carry it).

Order on the web through:

    Amazon.com

    Audible.com

    Barnes & Noble

    Books-A-Million

    www.LOL4.net for autographed copies

If you already have a copy of one or more of her books and would like an autographed bookplate for it, email her with your snail mail address and how many you need. She will get them off to you. And thank you!

End Notes

[i] "Creativity." *Merriam Webster*, Merriam Webster, www.merriam-webster.com/dictionary/creativity. Accessed 6 Oct. 2020.

[ii] Khalil, Radwa, et al. "The Link Between Creativity, Cognition, and Creative Drives and Underlying Neural Mechanisms." *Frontiers in Neural Circuits*, vol. 13, no. 1, 2019, pp. 1–16. *Frontiers*, doi:10.3389/fncir.2019.00018/full.

[iii] *IUPUI*. bradbury.iupui.edu/pages/bradburys-office/index.php. Accessed 6 Oct. 2020.

[iv] *The Hattiesburg Area Daylily Society*. www.hattiesburgdaylily.com. Accessed 4 Oct. 2020.

[v] Nelson, Connie. "Copy a Painting by an Old Master: Improve Your Art at the Museum." *Explore-Drawing-and-Painting.Com/*, 2019, www.explore-drawing-and-painting.com/copy-painting-in-museum.html.

[vi] "Through the Rijksmuseum With a Pencil." *Rijksmuseum*, www.rijksmuseum.nl/en/press/press-releases/through-the-rijksmuseum-with-a-pencil. Accessed 28 Sept. 2020.

[vii] "The Place They Do Imagineering." *Alcoa Aluminum*, graphic-design.tjs-labs.com/show-picture?id=1118935951&size=FULL. Accessed 6 Sept. 2020.

[viii] Ewald, Laura Anne. "The Everyman Puppet Theatre." *YouTube*, Laura Anne Ewald, 13 Mar. 2020, www.youtube.com/channel/UCkYObjlEJYk4pQljkElXqZw.

[ix] "JD Farms." *Https://Jdfarms.Us/*, jdfarms.us. Accessed 5 Nov. 2020.

[x] *Abita Mystery House and the UCM Museum in Abita Springs Louisiana.* abitamysteryhouse.com. Accessed 9 Jan. 2021.

[xi] *Hattiesburg Pocket Museum.* Hattiesburg Convention Commission, hattiesburgconventioncommission.com/hattiesburg-pocket-museum. Accessed 21 Mar. 2021.

[xii] NOMA. "Hercules the Archer." *New Orleans Museum of Art*, 4 June 2020, noma.org/collection/hercules-the-archer.

[xiii] Ohio State University. "This is your brain detecting patterns: It is different from other kinds of learning, study shows." ScienceDaily. ScienceDaily, 31 May 2018.

[xiv] Rogers, K. (2021, January 21). *Did You Know There's a "Little Grand Canyon" in MS? Mississippi Farm Country.* https://msfarmcountry.com/travel/attractions/did-you-know-theres-a-little-grand-canyon-in-ms/

[xv] "Psychology and Smell." *Fifth Sense,* www.fifthsense.org.uk/psychology-and-smell. Accessed 5 Jan. 2021.

[xvi] "The Science of Taste & Nutrition –." *Kerry Health And Nutrition Institute,* khni.kerry.com/taste/the-science-of-taste-nutrition/#:%7E: Accessed 10 Jan. 2021.

[xvii] Forman, Michael. "The Importance of Play in Adulthood." *Wanderlust,* 18 Sept. 2018, wanderlust.com/journal/the-importance-of-play-in-adulthood/#:%7E:

[xviii] "The Science." *National Institute for Play,* 5 Nov. 2020, www.nifplay.org/science/overview.

[xix] Evans, David. "Laugh Your Way to Creativity." *Psychology Today,* 8 Nov. 2017, www.psychologytoday.com/us/blog/can-t-we-all-just-get-along/201711/laugh-your-way-creativity.

[xx] Maxine. "Laughter Fuels Creativity." *Creative You Learning Lab,* 3 June 2020,

www.creativeyoulearninglab.com/laughter-fuels-creativity. /

[xxi] "Does Laughing Promote Creativity? – Psych2Go." *Psych2go.Net*, psych2go.net/laughing-promotes-creativity. Accessed 3 Oct. 2020.

www.ingramcontent.com/pod-product-compliance
Lightning Source LLC
LaVergne TN
LVHW021120080426
835510LV00012B/1767